ESCHPE IN TIME

ESCAPE IN TIME

EVETTE ROBERTS

RN, RM, LLB HONS, LPC, BTEC/FINANCE

With a Foreword
By
Rhesa Khezial

authorHOUSE®

AuthorHouse™
1663 Liberty Drive
Bloomington, IN 47403
www.authorhouse.com
Phone: 1-800-839-8640

© 2013 by Evette Roberts. All rights reserved.

No part of this book may be reproduced, stored in a retrieval system, or transmitted by any means without the written permission of the author.

Published by AuthorHouse   08/02/2013

ISBN: 978-1-4772-4274-2 (sc)
ISBN: 978-1-4772-4275-9 (e)

Any people depicted in stock imagery provided by Thinkstock are models, and such images are being used for illustrative purposes only.
Certain stock imagery © Thinkstock.

This book is printed on acid-free paper.

Because of the dynamic nature of the Internet, any web addresses or links contained in this book may have changed since publication and may no longer be valid. The views expressed in this work are solely those of the author and do not necessarily reflect the views of the publisher, and the publisher hereby disclaims any responsibility for them.

CONTENTS

Acknowledgement vii

Foreword ix

1. The Village Girl 1
2. Tying the Knot at Nineteen 19
3. Landing in the UK 25
4. Stepping Up 33
5. Moments of Pain 61
6. Timely Escape 75

ACKNOWLEDGEMENT

My desire to write this book started since 1997 as a midwife. This was before I faced some hardship in my forties, at the peak of my career. I wrote sections of the book sporadically, with the intention to complete it at the achievement of a major milestone in my life. In essence, no time is right as a number of developments are constantly emerging as part of the entire discourse. This book makes interesting reading especially for health professionals of all races and backgrounds.

I would like to give special thanks to the following people who have made it possible to write this book;–my parents (John Skelsha and Virginia Sebastien), Uncle Emrod Sebastien, siblings (Lucia, Riviere, Douglas, Celia, Lucky, Mervin and Ruth), Uncle Tony George and family, Uncle Peter George and family and Aunty Myrtle Wright.

Special thanks to my husband–Simpson Roberts and my two boys–Micah and Caleb Roberts who have been extremely supportive through my peaks and troughs.

Most importantly, the greatest praise and thanks are directed to the most Sovereign one; Jehovah Jireh (God, my Provider).

FOREWORD

The Commonwealth of Dominica is one of the smallest islands in the Caribbean, which gained independence from Great Britain on 3 November 1978, but it continues to provide and export a large number of intellectuals. Migrating from the Caribbean as an adult to the UK, whether for work or family reasons was a huge challenge almost 30 years ago as seen in the 1948's wind rush and this persisted decades later.

Another aspect of the Caribbean culture which remained intact several decades later is the drive, determination and ambition to be successful. There have been several outstanding nurses and midwives from several countries including the Caribbean who have enriched the National Health Service (NHS). This rich ethnic and multicultural mixture of healthcare staff reflects the equal multicultural blend in society.

Migration to the UK in 1988, almost 10 years after Dominican independence showed that acceptance and integration into the British culture had improved but more needed to be done. This book showed that persistence and sheer hard work proved the key to success. The Caribbean family values have shone through in this story. It provides motivation for adults who have recently migrated to the UK, not just for those coming from the Caribbean.

However after years in the NHS, the challenges of integration and progression to the managerial level required a herculean effort, and a daily renewal and reliance on one's spiritual strengths to cope under sometimes seemingly impossible conditions. The strength and academic prowess of the Caribbean spirit always shines through, especially for those coming from humble beginnings.

The Caribbean and British share a common passion for athletics and sports. With this being the Olympics year in London 2012, the opening ceremony celebrated the contribution of Caribbean immigrants in the wind rush and an even more significant contribution of the NHS. As one celebrates the successes of this adopted country individuals from different ethnic backgrounds continue to make a contribution to achieve medals. After the Olympics, one hopes that this momentum will generate long term acceptance and create more opportunities in the British society.

Rhesa Khezial

CHAPTER 1

CHAPTER 1

The Village Girl

Born in one of the smallest islands along the Caribbean Sea, I was one of seven children. We lived in the village of Colihaut along the West Coast and near enough to the sea. My mother was a housewife and my father; a well-known farmer and fisherman. All three girls and four boys spent many hours in a Baptist Church where our mother was a Sunday school teacher. Our half–sister also lived along the West Coast, in another village, approximately half an hour away.

My memories of the events leading to the birth of my last two siblings are so vivid that I can only say that women in the village were extremely strong and brave. My mother's usual line after a period of labour pain was; "call the nurse".

We all attended the village nursery (Cacarat), followed by the primary school. It was there we learnt a catalogue of rhymes like 'Row Row, Row Your Boat', 'Tyre, Tyre Standing There' and lots more. For such a small village, change of nursery location was somewhat excessive. I asked Jesus to come into my heart at eight years old, through the ministry of an American Missionary during Sunday school and have never turned my back on my faith. In fact, I have grown from strength to strength and completely unmoveable.

Equivalent to church routine was the expectation to go to the *height* (garden) with our parents. This was a task in itself, having to take public transport which was hugely sparse, or travel by foot (without shoes on many occasions) for at least ten miles. On numerous occasions, we stopped along the journey to address a small sharp piece of rock which had suddenly found its way under our feet causing severe pain. Did we have any choice but to continue the journey?

Travelling to the garden was public humiliation especially as a high school girl. I felt extremely embarrassed at the fact that while high school children flagged the public buses on a Saturday to travel to the town, I together with my parents and older siblings flagged the dumpers and pick-up trucks to take us to our destination. Returning from the garden late afternoon, invariably accompanied the carrying of some unbearable load on our heads for at least half an hour, until we arrived at the main road to again recommence the routine of flagging down public transport or walking the several miles home.

Imagine a bunch of green bananas or plantains, or even a tied bag of produce (dasheen, vegetables, oranges), or a basket of fruits! Such a painful and embarrassing experience! As adults, we (siblings) have often laughed at the times when we fell over several times with the fruits and produce making their way at no less than one hundred miles an hour down the cliff as we tripped, trying to navigate the narrow, bush-covered tracks.

"Make sure you do not drop the bananas, because one bruised banana, and the depot (banana plant) will reject the whole bunch"; my father would repeat to me when he placed the bunch on my head on a make–shift pad made from dry banana leaves. This was routine on 'Banana Day' as the depots in strategic places in specific villages were receiving the best bananas for exportation to a number of countries such as England. I was well known to be the feeblest amongst the children as I always found the issue of carrying load was extremely painful and that which required a herculean effort.

While we were not considered poor, my parents were extremely strict. My father in particular was one of principle and maintained that people should not have "so much clothes and shoes". We dared not ask for these items if he could see that the dress worn to church last Sunday was in perfect condition.

Fashion, dancing, listening to music, going to the beach, watching others dance and more were seen as carnal and destructive to the mind. Admittedly, we never lacked food or drink although memories of the occasional bread and butter with a cup of lime-leaves tea remain a reality

Conversely, he considered that girls should be clean, maintain cleanliness in the home, experts at cooking and washing, but the boys would be responsible for assisting with fishing and undertaking manual tasks. I held little interest in cooking as a teenager and could not claim any fame to a favourite dish of mine. We each took turns going to the market in town (Roseau), with my mother who sold a variety of produce like oranges, grapefruit, plantain, soft yam (Caplarw), ginger, breadnut and nutmegs. For me, this was most embarrassing and I hated the thought.

My mother used to shout; "Come and buy my oranges, lovely grapefruits, two for a dollar but lady–just give me one dollar". I really did not enjoy such demeaning practices and I saw it as a form of begging. What became even more embarrassing was when the shoppers passed by our produce on the market ground and bought the same produce from the lady stationed next to us, either because the price was cheaper or for some other reason.

Other embarrassing moments were examples of traders selling all their produce in a short space of time, leaving us to struggle on in the market. I used to find any excuse to go to the toilet especially in those days when the sun was blazing hot and there was practically no shelter. I viewed the whole ordeal as a form of begging. It must be said too that I had a sense of joy when we sold all our produce and more so, when this was done within a couple hours of settling in any market space one could find at the time.

Ice cream always followed by course and in those days, ice cream was ice cream; tasty, delicious, scrumptious and unforgettable. Of course my father took no part in going to the market as he was largely responsible for producing all this food, having spent several hours, weeding, digging, planting and watering his crops.

Travelling to the town for other matters was rare but was the most exciting time for us as children. Our 'nice' clothes and shoes were prepared the night before and invariably, we had very little sleep because of the excitement and having to wake up so early to catch the village truck or bus. The passengers used to laugh and speak a lot and that formed part of the excitement. Although they were all going on different missions, this sort of excitement was not exclusive to children. We often returned home with goodies such as corn curls, sweets, biscuits and toys and more exciting was the odd occasion when we acquired a new shoe, bag for school, uniform or church clothes.

Another significant practice was my dad going out to fish mainly on Saturdays. My mother timed his return by walking down to the seaside to assist with bringing the boat unto the shore and putting the fish into different bags by categories. On carrying the fish home following a five to seven minutes' walk, my dad would blow a shell to give the villagers an indication that fish was then on sale.

Again, it was a form of market where people were demanding and sort of fighting to buy the biggest red fish. As for me, I tried to hide upstairs and almost always covered my ears so as not to hear the open criticisms by some of the villagers that my dad was not selling the bigger fish, even when he tried to be fair by mixing both small and big and not favouring any person over the other.

Patois (broken French) was the second language which I recall was never taught, but naturally learnt by children. However, this language was not always welcomed by certain sections in the village. It is a shame that considering the island of Dominica sits between two French islands (Martinique and Guadeloupe), that we were not taught French as part of growing up.

I recall my dad being the breadwinner and controlled the purse strings while my mum, (the cook, cleaner, washer, nurse and representative at school), would have to make a very convincing case to be successful in the ultimate purchase of new shoes and clothes for us. He believed in saving and only using money if it is absolutely necessary. He was and still is a strong believer in being highly educated. Our house was constantly bombarded with comparative stories of children which he believed performed better at school.

My dad was of course displeased when my older brother decided not to sit the Common Entrance exam for entrance into High School. As the only child of seven who attended and completed High School in the Caribbean, there was enormous pressure on me to get the highest marks in the class. My parents sacrificed so much for me to attend High School and paying for the daily commute by bus. They went the extra mile to ensure that my secondary school journey was seamless even if it resulted in financial hardship. Books, shoes and uniform were extremely expensive. It almost goes without saying that I did not want to eat the ordinary food anymore- no more green banana and fish! I owe my parents so much for their huge sacrifice and I am extremely grateful.

There were invariably no compliments on passing any exam, unless the mark was higher than every child in the class especially classmates from the same village. My memories of High School was one where village girls at the Convent High School were not regarded on the same level as those from prestigious families in the town, and exams results in general were in their favour.

While spanking was not a regular occurrence in our household, I remember my beatings quite well indeed. The reasons in my opinion were so basic that I often seriously analysed them after the fact. I am sure most kids undertake this post mortem exercise after a slap or extended form of discipline culminating in a mental decision on how to react to the perpetrator for some time after the event. Fortunately, this never lasted for more than a few hours. Surely those questions around where your next plate of food would originate from only motivated us to fall in line very quickly, as angry as you were at the time.

"Go upstairs", a compelling command from my mother instilled such fear in me that knowing what was to follow could only serve to dismantle every ounce of quietness in my physical and emotional state. What was it about? I went to the river to wash some laundry for my neighbour before undertaking some chores at home for which I had received specific instructions. The beating on the day in question was so unique that all I remember saying was–"Mammy, Mammy, Mammy, I will not do it again". It was like as if the woman took pleasure in landing the belt or whip or shoe or any of her usual weapons she used to execute punishment.

Many children of my generation would relate to the times when our parents prepared themselves to execute judgement that they would sometimes say–"*Long I holdin this for you*" or "*Long time you lookin for it*". In this present day, this would be classified as 'child abuse'. However, I have conceded that this was the way parents disciplined in those days; the way they knew best and I truly respected my parents in every sense of the word. In many ways, discipline did me much good and I am thankful to God for them.

My only close and unrelated friend attended the same High School and I only saw her at school. My siblings and I were not allowed to visit friends in the village and we were encouraged to emulate our dad by almost adoring his parents, to the extent that like him, we spent several hours with our grandfather (Papa Alton), who was already pretty elderly. His death at one hundred and twelve left a huge void in my dad's life and as he grew older, we saw similar traits emerging like enjoying being in his bed even during the day.

My grandparents were loving and extremely protective of us all. Although they lived apart during my lifetime before their deaths, they each played a significant role in the lives of my siblings and I. Mam Inese always owned a grocery shop and there was not one day on passing her way that she would not offer cooked food or some delicacies. As generous as she was, she often told us that we were sinking her because many times we would ask her for finger foods which she would have had for sale. After all, she was our granny and I saw no problem with asking or taking from her.

As for Papa Alton, the man was excellent; so calm and gentle and as generous as my granny. One thing I remember is that they never asked about each other and we never saw this as strange as I suppose that's the setting we knew from childhood.

While befriending people was not encouraged in our household, what was heavily encouraged was having a close bond and respectful approach to the extended family especially to those who were highly regarded due to their occupation/profession. These family members, 'The Sebastiens' (and those who while they carried other surnames, were a branch of the same family) were mainly teachers, head teachers and nurses; professions of high esteem.

Our strict upbringing and regular attendance at church services were renowned in the village, but this did not deter my brothers at different stages from being truant in seeking girls during their teenage years. This displeased my parents enormously but the villagers sometimes reminded my dad (aka Speedy), of his sporty years following his return from England in the 1960's and well known for playing 'Loving Justice' (his favourite music) regularly in his shop, otherwise known as CABARWAY. While my parents did not demonstrate their love for us by kissing, stroking, and hugging, they did so in many other ways and never once did I doubt that they loved us, even in the midst of harsh discipline.

As children, we also had some great times and some more enjoyable than I can remember decades later. We flung stones at mangoes hanging on mango trees, killed and roasted birds, made small toys like paper boats and kites, telephones from empty match boxes and whistles from green coconut leaves. It was great fun! I love mangoes to this day and would spend any amount of money to purchase ripe, sweet Caribbean mangoes. Call it an addiction; so let it be. At least it is neither drugs nor alcohol.

A box of ripe Julie mangoes.

This village girl attended the Convent High School in the capital–Roseau. Following transfer from the village school to a Christian school in a nearby village namely; St Joseph, I passed the Common Entrance, one of the very few. To date, I am uncertain of the real benefits of the transfer but appreciate the rationale, albeit highly political.

My first day at High (Secondary School) in September 1979 is a hugely memorable one. In August of the same year, Hurricane David lashed the Commonwealth of Dominica to some destruction. The accessible roads for travel to the various parts of the island were barely accessible by vehicle or foot and the only means of transportation from my village to the next, southward was via canoe (*Carnot*-in our dialect). This was the most frightening experience for me especially having developed a phobia of boats. I blame my eldest brother–Riviere, who played risky games when we travelled by boat to the garden on the rare occasions.

I spent the first school year with my cousin, (Uncle Matthew George) who fully supported my parents and I by lodging me during the week. It was a refreshing time and full of laughs but loaded with great spiritual and educational advice, by both him and his late wife. It is appropriate at this point to express my heart–felt thanks for his enormous contribution to my upbringing, education and spiritual life.

My dad's constant reminders to respect all our extended family members, meant that we had a high degree of respect which could be interpreted as fear. Their contribution during our childhood days was also extremely significant and as a child, I remember receiving regular twenty dollar notes from Nurse Pascal Sebastian (Cousin Nurse), and her late brother and regular gifts from another cousin; also a Head Teacher. At the time of writing (September 2012), Cousin Nurse was 96 years old.

As for my grandparents, they were consistently involved in our lives and we were extremely close. Their deaths in 1992 (two weeks apart), left a rather large gap for some time. Thankfully, the positive memories outweigh the negatives.

Due to my strict upbringing, my extra-curricular activities were predominantly within the church youth group. As an avid reader, I enjoyed reading the bible (King James Version) and memorising verses especially in readiness for the bible quiz at the weekly youth meetings. Hanging out with other youths after the meetings was not regarded by my parents as best practice and as sure as light follows day, my mother regularly walked the street on Saturday evenings at a time she knew I would be returning home with the youth group who would invariably stop at a point to chat and entertain each other with jokes.

A common command given to me by the group was:–"Run Evette–child your mother coming". As quick as a flash, I would find the quickest route home. Why did she always embarrass me in this way and give me such little freedom?

My mother blamed dad who moaned increasingly at her when I was away from the home. Being away from home simply meant; being in the village on an errand or at youth meetings. Summer camps were most enjoyable but weekly youth meetings topped it for me. It was during those times that I developed an affinity for a young man who was my rival at the youth competitions. Initially, I could not stand one bone in his body and being my opponent, it just fed the dislike within me. It certainly was not love at first sight but after several sights.

Listening to secular music was discouraged in our home as well as in the church. In essence, we were required to learn all the old hymns and choruses, completely ignoring all other genres. This did not stop me from hearing non gospel songs which were being played daily while commuting to and from school. Even today, these secular songs especially from the greatest Calypsonians are constantly ringing in my head. Occasionally, my sudden desire to hear these songs, invariably move me to listen once again with some unreal excitement for a brief moment. Undoubtedly, these exercises always bring fond memories of those good old days.

I loved reading books and I had a serious addiction for new books. Storybooks were my favourite and I read so much that I knew I had to stop when I developed serious headaches. Headaches were severe on most occasions and I could only describe them as a knife slicing my body. One Sunday evening I stayed home and did not attend the evening service. I spent the two hours hugging a pillow and being wrestles on a chair. At one point, I had a vision to go to the seaside which was about five minutes from my house to drown myself to end this headache and this I have not shared with anyone to this day. It was not long before my parents returned home and further home remedies were applied with prayer until eventually I got some relief and went to bed.

As for self-image, I was a nerd I suppose. My clothes were not always well fitting and if I did have a 'nice' dress it fitted me to my figure. I admired my own figure with a thin waist, wide hips and a protruding derriere. I recall borrowing my cousin's clothes on some occasions for the purpose of church services. How embarrassing was that? My dresses were often homemade, first made by an older relative who of course was not contemporary and oh, did some people not have a good laugh! Some parts of the dresses were bigger and longer of course out of place.

Later on as a teenager, I was sent to the neighbouring village where a dressmaker would make me more modern dresses but these were rare occasions as one must remember that we were a large family; many mouths to feed and bodies to clothe. While I am thinking of this, I just want to completely block this off my mind by an act of omission. However by doing so, the pieces of the puzzle will certainly be missing, defeating the object of my book.

Carnival festival was an annual event with young men in the village disguising themselves with various masks and matching/dancing round the village. Rarely did we recognise the men but we certainly knew the difference between men and women. There were at least one or two women who joined the group each year. Carnival was exciting but at the same time, very frightening as the men sometimes flung bottles while they matched and the event was sometimes used as a platform for vengeance.

Well, we cooked a lot of red fish, dasheen, green bananas, yams, rice, macaroni and cheese pie and the favourite was Dumpling, Peas and Jel (DPJ). This was a combination of kidney beans with pumpkin, very hard dumplings and pig's mouth (substituted for any other meat). My dad kneaded the dumplings so hard that on biting, the dry flour and or cornmeal would disperse into the air. It is my understanding that the other villages were not familiar with this dish, but one could argue that the island's staple dish; Mountain Chicken (frog), was also not familiar to the natives.

While we had no television, we kept ourselves thoroughly entertained through games, jokes, reading, playing swimming, making popcorn, catching birds and eating super fruits like mangoes, paw paw, sugar apples, sour sop and roasted corn. Christmas was exciting as there was a special atmosphere and one which was surreal. We stayed up very late at nights singing Christmas carols. We cooked salted meat in dumplings and Red (Kidney) beans and drank our homemade special drinks like Guinness pinch and Sorrel.

Exchange of gifts and giving out cards were rather rare and we mostly enjoyed the special church services and parties to mark the event and welcome the New Year. This was what I regard as proper celebration of Christmas rather than the commercialised version I witness in the United Kingdom. This is the main reason for extricating ourselves from the thrills and buzz of the event as the focus should be the birth of Jesus; the one who was sent to save the world.

The real trigger was buying a gift for a distant member of my family on my first Christmas in the UK. She quickly returned the gift with no explanation and you can imagine the grave embarrassment. I can only imagine that she did not like the silver set and was probably expecting a Rolls Royce from a 20 year old who had only just arrived in the country as an economic migrant. We would say in Dominica:-'you were too fast!'

CHAPTER 2

CHAPTER 2

Tying the Knot at Nineteen

My teenage years were spent largely at school and church and consumed with family and quality time with episodes of laughter among my siblings. On completion of my High School education at eighteen, I taught at the local primary school. I fell in love with that young Christian man who was British by birth. Although I concealed the relationship for the best part of one year, revealing my true love as a teenager was unwelcomed especially by my father. He wanted me to marry someone with a known profession and not a hospital casual worker who on some occasions spent his spare time on fishing boats pulling nets, in an attempt to catch fish with the local fishermen.

Periodic family meetings which included my future husband, called by my parents were often sessions of interrogations to ascertain whether our relationship was right. They quickly took control, planned a date for our engagement and ushered us into the planning of our wedding. Well, this came as a real shock! Was I ready for living with a man before the age of twenty? What did I know about keeping house and pleasing a man? Whether I liked it or not, I was getting married as according to my dad, "no child will bring shame to my house". This shame referred to any Christian girl falling pregnant outside marriage.

We planned our wedding with support and assistance from family members. Aunties and Uncles were largely abroad in England or one of the French islands within the Caribbean. My uncle Emrod (my father's brother) who resided in England was our favourite as he regularly sent money at Christmas time. Now in his early 70's, he remains the favourite as he is exceptionally caring, ambitious, hardworking and business-minded.

The wedding was scheduled for 28 December 1985, in our small village, with hand written invitations to church folks, family and friends. My husband and I had little money and I first recognised my planning skills and ability to budget when I took control of organising the wedding. My Pastor (Emanuel Parillon) was instrumental in the planning and success of the wedding service and ceremony; his wife being equally supportive.

My Aunt Mary (mother's sister) was so gentle, loving, full of fun and laughter and extremely helpful and supportive especially at this special time for me. Sadly, she passed away as I write this book, at 75 years old (2012). Although had diabetes and a heart condition, she passed away in hospital in the Caribbean, under suspicious circumstances.

My husband's parents were residing in England and their relationship was strained from childhood and therefore their contribution was not particularly significant. Most family members immediate, extended, far and near supported in their own little way.

We ordered the cake from the infamous *Francs* shop in the town and ashamedly could not pay the full amount on collection. After much pleading, the owner agreed that we MUST return with payment the week following the event. What did we get ourselves into at our age?

My wedding dress was of course hired but I was pleased that I chose it myself. The only wedding ring (bridal) we could afford was fourteen caret gold and paid for by instalments. In planning ahead in terms of living accommodation, we debated whether to temporarily live with my parents or rent a property. Prior to the wedding, we were certain that living alone would be the better option.

The wedding went as planned with a large number of uninvited villagers gathering outside the Baptist Church building. It was a memorable day as two very young people tied the knot at such a tender age, with some prior marriage counselling, little exposure and experience in intimacy together, and basically, no idea of what to expect once the wedding celebrations had ended on that day.

Due to limited finance, there was no plan for honeymoon in any shape or form, but we continued as normal with very little discussion on having children. One can imagine that we had to learn many new things without assistance or coaching from others. The village nurse can vouch for my ignorance as I attended her clinic in a panicked state when I was rather concerned about a discharge. Little did I know; intimacy comes with a residual price!

Being married meant there was some expectation that children would shortly follow. This certainly was not our short-term plan. I felt quite 'wifey' though as the deep desire to do the household chores and please my husband in terms of having a clean house and cooking daily meals overwhelmed me to satisfaction. What I have never expressed publicly is the embarrassment of living in a small, old wooden house with an outside pit toilet, plagued with the nastiest insects–cockroaches. My phobia of cockroaches increased phenomenally and the site of this black, big, horrible and frightening insect caused me to literally scream and run for my life.

I can only attribute the root cause of my gruelling fear of cockroaches to my childhood days; while regularly sitting on our outside pit toilet, these insects used to crawl up the sides and up my derrière! Just writing these words is causing goose pumps all up my skin–an experience I wish never to encounter again in my lifetime.

Less than one year into the marriage, my husband returned to the United Kingdom where I would subsequently join him. Our reunion ensued six months later. The six months without my husband was a time of grave emotional hardship as we had grown so close together. Letter writing became my hobby with strong words describing the impact of his absence on me and that I needed to be rescued from a strange type of loneliness, despite living with my parents and siblings.

He often reminded me that my letters were extremely frequent for which he received regular reminders from his dad who regarded such an act as distasteful. Did this bother me in the least? Not at all, as I was not married to him, but to his son!

CHAPTER 3

CHAPTER 3

Landing in the UK

Entering the United Kingdom, such a huge country, was incomparable to the island of Dominica with a population of 60,000. It was indeed a culture shock in several ways; joining my husband who was himself trying to acclimatise to a country he had left as a toddler, learning a new culture and getting used to being away from my parents and siblings, and eating foods which were completely alien. I was certainly determined not to change my Dominican accent and maintained what I had been taught as *Standard English* at primary and secondary school, even though this meant that my accent was 'rough', 'harsh', 'abrupt' and 'heavy' in the eyes of a British society.

Eating mashed potatoes was likened to eating dog's vomit and foods classified as deserts;–the gateaux, rice pudding, semolina, sliced roast meat and English tea were never going to form part of my daily life. Of course I was not quintessentially British!

I had to adjust to a new environment, new church, and new food and play the role of wife under these new circumstances. However, being a passionate person with ambition for development and progress, I was not ready to sit at home at age 20 and bearing children each year. My husband and I were kindly assisted by my only maternal uncle in the UK as he 'put us up' for a short period of time while we tried to settle as a couple. We are extremely grateful to him for this transition. Although money was not in abundance, we used this opportunity to put our minion plans into action.

Sundays were spent in church services followed by visits to my close family members. My husband continued his battle in seeking favour from his family and slowly and tentatively they engaged with him in insignificant bursts. Undoubtedly, he was embraced by my extended family who accepted him to the degree that I felt then and still feel today that he is the 'favourite'. He was deemed as gentle, quiet, kind and friendly, completely opposite to my qualities, in their eyes.

As homesick as I was, constantly needing to find a phone box to speak with my parents; I found solace in close relatives in the UK. In those days, there were no mobile phones and using the landline to telephone abroad was extremely expensive. Those who have migrated to the United Kingdom from the West Indies, Africa and far flung lands can relate to the sound of the coins being swallowed in the phone booths at a very rapid pace, causing much heartbreak.

I was so determined to be a success at a profession; especially Nursing. My favourite paternal uncle (Emrod) who was such an encourager. He gave us all the tools needed to push ourselves to a level where we became self-sufficient. Our regular Sunday visits always culminated in a litany of advice on key topics such as the wise use of money, striving to be a homeowner and grabbing all opportunities to work. One must admit that as much as it sometimes felt like a broken record, it was the best advice which served us well to this very day. Walking several miles on a Sunday afternoon, only a few weeks of landing in the United Kingdom to find a Nursing Agency in Wanstead was a strong indicator that I was determined to make quick and significant progress. It was an extremely worthwhile walk as it culminated in the start of Agency work as an Auxiliary nurse at various hospitals and Nursing Homes; a start to a brighter future.

It was no laughing matter when I woke up in the early mornings trying to find hospitals and Nursing homes to undertake shifts assigned by the Agency. I could tell numerous stories about these old days. It was a very cold winter morning while walking a long distance from the bus stop to the hospital before 7am. In my naivety, I was walking so bold and brave and totally in my own world. Halfway through the long walk, I felt an impregnated silence like something was wrong; a completely weird feeling!

I was prompted to turn behind and as I did so, I was shocked to find a tall young man tugging at my bag which was partly tucked under my right arm. Honestly, I was in such shock that as much as I wanted to scream, nothing came out of my much. When I pulled away from the young man, he quickly ran away ahead of me into thin air. As frightened as I was, my main concern was to get to work to earn some money knowing that we were jointly earning just enough to eat and drink at this stage. After all, I was not hurt and just wanted to get to work. Thereafter, I was much more vigilant and where possible, my husband travelled with me at nights and early mornings.

One of the most embarrassing moments was turning up at a hospital for work in ordinary clothes. I was bold indeed to even venture into this environment with no previous experience or exposure. It was the first hospital shift having worked mainly in Nursing homes as a Care Assistant.

On reporting to the Nursing Officer, she asked me in the most abrupt tone–"Where is your uniform?" Well, only if the ground could swallow me up! No one had informed me of the requirement to wear a uniform. She was having none of it and told me in no uncertain terms that I should return home as I cannot work in her department without uniform.

Shame-faced, I slowly walked out of the ward, embarrassment overwhelmed me and I felt so worthless. Could she not have been kinder to me? However, with hindsight, I was glad I did not stay on because the state these patients was in lying on those beds, would be enough to put me off any form of nursing. I believe God had a hand in this situation.

My way of doing things took a while to change inside and outside the home as acclimatisation was progressive and far from instant. Walking down the street with a plastic cap over my '*jerry curl*' (curly perm), looking back–was crazy. Covering my head with a plastic bag, if caught by rain unprepared was also grotesque as naivety prevailed in those days of innocence. What possessed me to believe that a shopkeeper would allow me to use his toilet at six thirty in the morning on my way to work?

I was convinced that when I did have children, they would only speak like me with no exposure to cockney and junk food and sweets. With no thanks to my close family members especially Aunty Bernice's daughters who constantly remind me that I was convinced that even my children would have no problems with saying words such as BARLOON in my own dialect (correct pronunciation is 'balloon'). I refused to purchase a washing machine as felt this would just cause me to be lazy. In the absence of a river where I had the luxury of free flowing water and a choice of rocks to exercise the power of my strong hands as part of the rolling motion, I used buckets to wash the dirty laundry. I was still in the Caribbean mood!

Don't I remember those days and many would relate to similar stories in the Caribbean. Washing machines were unheard of and we all dreaded a Saturday–washing, cleaning and purging day. We took baskets of dirty laundry to the river where we stood for hours washing by hand and rolling our pieces of dirty garments.

Some women had their stones marked and you would have to give way to any one woman whose stone you had taken on that Saturday morning. Of course there was lots of gossip on who was pregnant, who aborted which number baby and when, but also those of us with sores of any type on our feet and legs, were tormented by the small fishes, especially the well-known one call Millet.

As a young girl, I loved catching crayfish and 'millet' in the river for fun. Most times we roasted these creatures and after a while we sold the 'millet' and other types of fish to the poorest of the villagers who would offer us something as small at a cent per each fish.

We formulated an opinion at a very small age that if 'millet' could pick at our sores, they were filthy and would make us most unhealthy. I loved rabbits and during my childhood days, I reared a few and continued to do so in the UK. The foxes soon had their way with my lovely pets on more than one occasion. I gave up this hobby mainly because of the constant need to clean the hutch on a regular basis.

The love shown by my extended family especially my uncles went a long way to assist me in settling into a new country. Often we hear people say that 'big countries' make Christians turn away from God. I was determined to prove people wrong and live a strong Christian life. My uncles; Peter and Tony were instrumental in that aspect of my life as they were and are still strong examples. Their practical input of hospitality and generosity can never be forgotten.

Much of our free time was spent with close family members when my husband and I were not travelling round the country familiarising ourselves with different parts of Britain. Our first experience of South Wales in the 90's was thoroughly enriching and we have taken such a shine to this particular countryside countryside, that we have developed friendships with owners of the hotels where we spent brief holidays.

Within a year of my arrival in the United Kingdom, we were living in shared accommodation with complete strangers and my cooking skills were further tested. By self-admission, I hated cooking and sought ways to reverse my approach. One of my cousins contributed significantly by supplying brand new books on various recipes. While I have mastered a number of recipes including my own, her baking is just second to none.

My husband was an avid cricketer and played for the Bow Rovers cricket team whose home ground was in West Ham Park in East London. His several trophies of his achievements as a left hand bowler and batsman are truly representative of his contribution to the game. It is unfortunate that he retired from cricket at forty years old–a man in his prime and so proficient at the game!

CHAPTER 4

CHAPTER 4

Stepping Up

Nursing was my profession as far as I was concerned but I love a lively debate and a healthy argument. Therefore, my eyes were also fixed on the legal profession. I had to start somewhere. Arrival in the UK with a few GCE's were not going to get me very far but I was determined to make it.

Thankfully, I have always had an inquisitive spirit and I used this to my advantage when leaving secondary school in 1984. I shadowed the District Nurse in my village for about six months, in spite of rejections from the Island's only Nursing School. In September of the same year, I started as an 'unqualified teacher' in the village primary school. I was so pleased for such an opportunity, but I would continue to dream of being a nurse.

It all started when a positive reference from the District Nurse (M.A) in Dominica was received by the Nursing Agency in the UK. Requests to fill shifts were consistent and I worked on the possibility of training to be a qualified nurse. Within nine months of arrival, I started my General Nurse training in 1988. This was the start of a long three and a half years of study and work. With no children in sight, I was able to fully concentrate on making this a real success.

The entire training days, months and years remain vivid in my mind; both the good and the bad. I also faced unpleasant comments from patients; the most famous being–"I don't want you to look after me-go back to your own country". As a student nurse, where do you turn, knowing full well that the likelihood of mental illness was extremely remote in this case?

Again, my so called anti-social ways were frowned upon by nurses who were themselves established in the profession; some of which gave me negative reports as mentors; social rather than clinical. I do remember challenging my Nursing Tutor by asking him to confirm whether the fact that I did not drink tea and sat with the qualified nurses in a smoked filled room would affect the final outcome of this course and my care towards patients. His response was the inevitable–"under no circumstances".

I qualified as a General Nurse in 1991, undertook a post registration nursing role and started the following day at the local hospital, in the Chest-Medical ward. What could be more frightening than on the first day, having to attend to a Cardiac Arrest situation? The adrenaline was pumping and I felt myself spinning; the classroom lectures became a blur and my heart was pumping too hard to maintain a clear mind. I managed to activate all the appropriate actions in a timely fashion but sadly, this man who was already quite unwell; passed away.

I commenced my midwifery training in the same year. This was a tedious eighteen months within a unique specialism. I became even more competitive and was determined to be top of my group, having been beaten by a Mauritian in my nursing group. I enjoyed all aspects of my training and of course, with every delivery of a baby without my mentor's hands on, was phenomenal. I looked forward to being an autonomous midwife, within a profession that seemed more fulfilling than nursing itself.

My midwifery training culminated in my first pregnancy at four months. I recall members of my group gathering in an office on one of the wards to receive our final exam results by telephone. Well, you can imagine the shouting and elation and the results I was really hoping for; to secure the highest mark. On graduation day (ten days following emergency caesarean section), I received a reward for the best student midwife on merit. It was my day!

Micah Andy Simpson Roberts was born in 1993 by caesarean section; eight years into the marriage. I cannot stress the _Trouble_ he gave before being surgically removed almost three weeks early. My husband can relate the horror stories surrounding the labour. Truthfully, I had exhausted the word 'Mammy'. How could my poor mother have heard these shouts coming from an operating room where a doctor was attempting to break my waters in a controlled environment?

What followed next was rather unpredicted as I was under the impression that the custom of automatic appointment at your training hospital was mandatory. Six weeks after the birth of our first boy, I restarted agency nursing and pursued a midwifery post at my hospital.

"Our midwifery jobs are for our students", said the Head of Midwifery in the corridor, in the presence of her colleagues, when I humbly asked whether there were vacancies. You can imagine how I felt on hearing her response. If only the ground would swallow me up! I returned to my house completely deflated, fearing that I will never remember what I learnt during my midwifery training.

A change of heart came when her colleague reprimanded her for the response, that the Head of Midwifery invited me to attend an interview on completion of an application form, for bank (locum) shifts. At the start of the interview, all three senior midwives made it absolutely clear that they would not be interviewing me for a permanent post. I went with the flow, knowing that man is not in control of my destiny but God.

During the interview, I was informed that I was putting the lot of them to shame–their words and not mine. I was discouraged from advancing myself in terms of doing further studies with the intention of becoming a midwifery tutor; certainly not in the short term.

A telephone call ensued, confirming that I had done so well at the interview that they were offering me a permanent post. Another exciting moment for me caused me to forget the degree of humiliation I faced to get there in the first place. The fact that I was now going to be called a Midwife was great and I was just so excited. I began revising my notes and visualising aspects of my practice especially in relation to labour and delivery. While I was eager to start, I had a baby who required minding while we both worked; my husband being an installation engineer for a security/alarm company in the City.

Child minding issues were quickly resolved and I started as a midwife in November 1993. Day one orientation flew out of the window when I faced a labour ward which was heaving with women and all different types of activities.

I quickly acclimatised and adapted to a profession which I had admired during my nurse training. I grew to love the role as a practising midwife, exercising what I believe was excellent and enviable skills; especially my detailed documentation, mentoring various groups of students and being in charge of different sections of the local maternity unit, on a shift by shift basis. Like many midwives, I was offered several gifts by families to whom I had provided care both in a junior and senior position. Some were rejected in order to comply with the Code of Conduct and local ethics.

The Delivery Suite was of course my preferred area of practice as it was always full of buzz and excitement of screams and laughter. Generally, as a team of midwives we worked together in the busy and quieter times; each looking out for the other and never waiting for one to ask for help. We saw each other's needs and acted with compassion. I remember baking cakes for us to consume on night duty and these went down as a treat. I can honestly say with confidence that this community spirit in midwifery begun to be eroded in the late 90's and what was such a fulfilling profession is one of hard work mentally, physically and emotionally.

That first day as a qualified midwife prepared me for some difficult shifts in the future. Being thrown into the deep end with no post registration experience matured me in every sense of the word. I quickly consolidated my learning and practised with caution at every level. Some aspects of midwifery I disliked and others I really liked until this day. Working with various midwives and doctors of differing backgrounds motivated me to examine my own cultural, spiritual and personal qualities, against societal factors displayed within the work environment.

Our second son, Caleb Rohan Alton Roberts was born three years later (1996) and we were certain this was our full contribution to the production line. Being conscious of the previous hardship with childcare, we invited my mother to travel from the Caribbean to the UK to assist for a few months. We were extremely grateful for the help and companionship.

As a very young boy, Micah developed an interest in cricket and was extremely excited about the prospect of playing in the same vicinity as his dad when we supported him during all his matches. However, eventually, football became the most appealing sport and he participated in various team matches. Caleb became a left hand bowler from the age of two and oh boy! What a pleasure it was to watch him play spin bowling. By the age of thirteen, he also grew increasingly interested in playing football to the extent that he made it clear that football was a chosen career rather than a hobby.

My Christian pilgrimage has been an uphill struggle against different forces and my upbringing has always made it impossible to retaliate or appear to be rude. Over the years, I viewed this as negative since in many circumstances, I would 'eat humble pie' when in fact I would be justified in my actions but others would be allowed to feel they have won.

As a young girl growing up in Dominica, I have always been taught to be polite, submissive, kind, docile and modest. A vivid memory is at age thirteen when I saw my first menarche. My mother quickly showed the pants to my dad and said to me in a firm voice;–"if you play with boys now, you will fall pregnant". A horrified look impregnated my face and deep within I knew that such talk was 'poppy cock' (excuse the British slang).

Working as a midwife in London meant that one came across various groups of patients, different due to culture, race, colour, background, religion and colleagues were categorised similarly.

I was always deemed to be very different and just too serious at work. I attended no social events and had little or no connection with work colleagues outside the work environment.

My work pattern changed to accommodate my boys who were very young and needed my attention, especially as the younger was breastfeeding until the age of one. My promotion to the position of senior midwife was an uplifting experience and I grew to further love the midwifery profession. Shift work was intense and the workload and patient/midwife ratio were unbelievable; so heavy that there was practically no strength to entertain social activities.

In August 1997, I was severely tortured by an unusual ear infection. It was my second consecutive night shift on the Delivery Suite. For those who know me well enough, I was determined to always own all the necessary equipment to undertake my tasks as a midwife. This included examples such as Pinards and stethoscope with each marked with my name and a warning–Do Not Touch!

On the first night, a member of staff borrowed my stethoscope and this was a very rare occasion. I do not recall cleaning the piece of equipment on its return as the level of activities during the shift was indescribable.

On the following night, just before midnight, I experienced gradual severe and excruciating pain in my right ear which worsened within a short space of time. The Co-ordinator duly released me to return home seven hours into the shift. I was then hospitalised the following day as the pain became worse and involved both ears at this stage. During my hospital stay, I wrote part of this book, giving a ball by ball commentary of events.

"To date, I have been in hospital for three nights, on intravenous antibiotics and regular oral and intramuscular pain killers; no real improvements! Truthfully, I can honestly say that I have never experienced such agonising, wicked, violent and excruciating pains like this, in and around both ears contemporaneously. In comparison, I would prefer to have a caesarean section performed many times over in one day; metaphorically speaking.

This brought many thoughts into my mind; impossible questions too! Have I wronged God? Have I neglected some vital aspects of my Christian life? Have I been receptive to God's voice lately or have I been failing to exercise faith with regards to family and professional matters? Why did I detract from my principle–do not let anyone borrow your stethoscope?

Leaving the spiritual side for the present, it is appropriate to mention the extraordinary characteristics and qualities of that special man in my life; for his unconditional support. The boys were well cared for, my basic needs were met, nothing seemed too hard for him to do and the boys basked in the joys of daddy's presence and pursued other avenues to seek more traces of his love, patience, endurance and meekness. We faced some trying times as we were unable to find suitable people to care for the boys during my hospitalisation.

A family friend assisted and this matter was quickly resolved until discharge from hospital.

I am extremely satisfied with the care at a local hospital and all health professionals involved in my care have exercised the highest level of professionalism. It is the fourth day in hospital and I am beginning to feel myself again. The pain has subsided but my hearing is somewhat impaired; hope temporarily. I am awaiting swab results and a date for discharge.

Nine hours into the day and I am suffering again and at the mercy of drugs. The Ear, Nose and Throat Specialist has looked into my ears this morning and unfortunately, confirmed the need for further treatment. I feel out of touch with society to some extent and I am surely surrounded by a different type of illness from the usual baby boom. I miss the boys especially the last boy; missing the different stages of development.

Gosh! I have just tasted the hospital food for the first time in four days. The best way to describe what I have tasted can be summarised as–SALT, SALT, SALT. It was Meat in Potato pie; type of meat was not specified. I pray God it is not Beef with the BSE/MAD Cow disease in season.

It's the afternoon of the fourth day and I was overwhelmed with visits from family and friends. I can assuredly say that my spirit was lifted, not to mention the edible things they brought along, namely; chips, mango (my favourite fruit), West Indian food and delicacies. However, what I longed for the most is to get out of here by tomorrow morning. No doubt I will return to the outpatient appointment. The new school term begins next week and I need to make the necessary arrangements to facilitate my four year old's commencement at nursery.

It's the next morning, it is cold and I am looking forward to hearing the words—"you may go home today". The long anticipated words rolled out of the doctor's mouth a few hours later on day five and I am so excited. I guess this brings closure to another chapter of my book".

Within two days of discharge, the sad news of Princess Diana hit the nation. It was a Sunday morning and on hearing the news while still asleep placed everything into perspective. How significant was a painful ear infection compared to such a tragic death of a well-known, well-loved and popular person. It was an extremely sad time.

I commenced a law degree at University (part-time), less than four weeks later and was convinced that the doctors failed to diagnose deafness as a complication of this drastic and aggressive ear infection. It became more noticeable during my lectures as I struggled to clearly hear all the lectures being delivered from the podium. In many ways, I mitigated by sitting at front seats at all lectures and seminars.

The first year at university was tedious especially working full-time as a midwife and caring for two young children. Reading law books, lengthy law reports and judgements, concentrated and condensed lectures and seminars required a deep sense of concentration as some parts were difficult to assimilate. Reference to the aspects of history and political events like the Holocaust completely lost me and I was left wondering how I would cope with playing catch-up. By the end of the first year, I was successful at all the exams and other forms of assessments. I give God all the praise and glory for his unfailing love.

My second brother got married in the UK and this was also an exciting moment for us all although the day was pretty cold. My youngest brother followed some years later. My parents must be extremely proud knowing that all but one child are now married and grandchildren are in abundance; spanning from various parts of the Caribbean, US Virgin Island and the UK.

Of course, two young children, a full time job and undertaking a major course of study in addition to short courses relating to work, I longed for days of reprieve. Interest at work was on the decline and both boys were becoming increasingly aggressive towards each other.

My time at home included lots of cooking and I longed for the day when both boys were in school full time, as it would remarkably reduce my hours in the kitchen where both boys loved to admire me in action up until the final product is handed to them. At one point, based on the daily chores at home and work, on a number of occasions I was inclined to change the title of this book to 'Servant, Maid, Cook, Cleaner, Foreman, Overseer, Skivvy, General Dog's Body'.

'It is July 1998 and we are preparing for a four week holiday in my birth country, Dominica (the last being 1994). My husband and I are literally counting our working days. Work continues to be stressful and we were pleased to be new members of a local church.

We had a great holiday, stress and complication free and returned in good spirits. Four weeks after our return we received news that my dad was taken Ill and had lost a considerable amount of weight. No definite diagnosis was given in spite of several tests and my dad was convinced that he had some sort of cancer. This devastated me especially while studying during the second year at university.

The nature of my work had also become more demanding and I viewed it as a chore. Plans were being made for our return as we feared the worse. His condition remained stable and on the same day of first January exam (1999), he underwent an operation which was later deemed as rather unnecessary. His recovery was remarkable and we were indeed relieved to receive such news.

Patients are getting more demanding, expectations increasing and midwives are losing all autonomy—is the best description of my observations within the world of midwifery and obstetrics. I feel very trapped and skills seriously stifled; there appears to be no scope for progression and I desperately need to find a way of escape. I proceeded to reduce my working hours in order that I had Sundays off to assist with Sunday school and other church work.

My first son was experiencing episodes of bullying at school with some emotional effects and frankly, the school mis-managed the *entire ordeal. Attempts were made to find him another school for fear of the complications and to avoid the domino effect of affecting his excellent intellectual skills which were already being stifled by the primary school. All attempts failed in securing the most appropriate school and we provided a high level of support for him while he remained at the current school.*

Summer time arrived and my second year at university culminated in excellent results. All praise to God Almighty–I can do all things through him. A viral infection mastered my battered body for about one week and thankfully I did not require hospitalisation. Conservative treatment was effective'.

At the end of Semester A of Year 2 at University, I was so mentally exhausted that I took off with my younger son on a two week holiday to Dominica for a well-deserved rest. Despite a number of problems with the airlines, we had a great and restful time. My husband did a marvellous job, caring for our six year old and the domestic affairs in the home. Returning to work was a chore and I felt unable to continue in the capacity as hospital midwife. It was time for change.

By February 2000, I was orientated into the community, working in a more autonomous capacity as community midwife. Mixed feelings flooded me as I could not imagine going into people's homes; some completely unappealing. How would I hide my feelings? Would I be able to exercise wisdom? I lacked diplomacy at the best of time! The thing is either black or white!

Third year exam results soared and I gave God continuous praise and thanks and to my husband who was so supportive and understanding. My parents visited us during the summer and it was the most fantastic time having such invaluable assistance from them with the kids and their presence filled our home with joy and laughter.

Community midwifery had both its advantages and disadvantages. While autonomy was a plus, there was the disadvantage of constantly feeling that one is never away from work. Week by week, running in between clinics and doing twenty four hour on calls did not go down very well with me. This was not what I desired to be part of my daily life for much longer. Being on call meant that one could be called to a house in any area and one completely alien.

On one particular night, my older brother was visiting while on a course of study in Holland. I was called out to assist a midwife at a homebirth at 21.30 hours. I had no clue where I was heading and I got lost most of the way. I eventually found the address, participated in the homebirth and returned home at 03:00 hours the following morning. My brother's exact words to me were:–"This job is dangerous . . . . how can you be out there at this time of night driving all alone?" This was certainly a wake–up call for me.

In summary, I was transferred back into the hospital setting, shortly after this experience. While the hospital environment was not ideal, after a year in the Community, I was prepared to try anything else at this stage. At this point, my eyes were opened to any opportunity which would bring about a change towards my progress and development. My greatest consolation at this time was the fact that I was coming towards the end of my law degree and hoping for greater things!

The time came in 2002 when I secured a 2.1 honours degree in law (LLB) and there were no words to describe my feelings in achieving such great success considering the nature of my work, caring for young children and being involved in church activities. Again, I gave God the praise as without him; I would not have achieved such success. My husband and boys were brilliant and we all had a common understanding over the years. I made a decision at the beginning of my studies, that in order to balance work, study and family life, I spent early evenings with the family and studied late into the night when everyone had gone to bed. This was a huge sacrifice but worked extremely well. My plan was to save sufficient funds to undertake the Legal Practice Course at Law School.

Sadly, work situation became worse where one felt so demoralised and the temptation was to seek out alternative employment. Having young children meant a constant feeling of being trapped, having to joggle shifts with uncertain childcare arrangements and the occasional sudden childhood illnesses. I needed to get out of this trap. There was something better out there for me than just coming into hospital to care for women before, during or after labour. I just needed a way out to exercise the other skills which came naturally or were learnt over the years.

In pursuing my dream to penetrate the legal career, I was successful in securing a job with the Crown Prosecution Service (CPS) in 2003. While this was an opportunity which gave me exposure to the courts and hands–on experience with preparing cases for criminal prosecution, it was clear that due to the heavy workload, it would not be conducive to continue working in this capacity and at the same time, undertake the Legal Practice Course even on a part-time basis.

Thankfully, I regained a post as a midwife at my previous hospital and enjoyed the work again. Interestingly enough, I worked as a midwife on an honorary contract throughout the time I was with the CPS and therefore was up to date with current practice.

My Legal Practice Course started in the same year and travel and studies complicated matters even more. This course was so much more intense, but like my law degree, I enjoyed most subjects and especially applying principles and past judgements to facts of cases/scenarios. I also completed the course and was indeed elated that again, the ordinary girl had made it! What more could I have asked for at this stage in my life in my early thirties? The crucial question was—What next?

The breakthrough at work came when I was successful at interview for a promotion in a specialist midwifery post; the first such title within the Organisation and chosen out of five candidates. What was to follow was unpredictable. The role was huge and almost limitless and of course in essence, name a problem and *'Evette will fix it'* was the approach by many.

I inherited a load of outstanding work and discovered my talent of Creator/Inventor of systems. Being an extremely organised person with a methodical approach to life, these skills only served to enhance my role. I supported staff of all grades on wards and departments, doctors and managers.

My experience in leading on a project undertaking different types of investigations, meeting with staff and patients/ families, working regularly as a midwife, travelling between two hospitals (sometimes more than once in a day), gave me wide exposure to unknown areas within obstetrics/maternity. Topics covered by reading a number of articles and during courses became a reality.

The constant flow of midwives to my office, meant that I constantly sacrificed my own commitments, but was willing to assist and support in the name of raising standards. This was commensurate with the ultimate goal of prevention of adverse incidents, being proactive rather than reactive.

As a nurse and midwife for over ten years by this time meant that I was predominantly on the shop floor–the wards; with no experience of management. My relationship with Consultant

Obstetricians, Paediatricians and Managers were purely related to patient care but being in this role, this changed immensely.

A healthy professional rapport developed with all staff and those in managerial positions. I quickly earned a high level of respect on a different level and although positive, this had its own disadvantage–little time to breathe *per se*. The workload was indeed insurmountable and good planning and time management meant I enjoyed a level of peace and satisfaction at the end of each day's work.

Covering two sites with a combined annual delivery rate greater than most in London, was a humongous task. I recall so clearly that for the first six months in post, there was no dedicated office for me to sit and undertake my duties on one of the two sites.

As fearless as I am naturally, I did not hesitate to humbly sit on the floor in the management office where all the administrative staff enjoyed comfortable seats with their own computers and adjoining kitchen. Members of the team walked over me as they proceeded with their daily tasks and it was not until two years ago that one of the secretaries hilariously recounted the events of those yester years. We used this time as a platform to reminisce about the old days.

They often asked each other as I left the office 'what is this mad woman doing sitting on the floor in our office?'. While my actions were not in protest, after some time, it achieved its aim and I was placed in an empty cupboard (small box room). Within a year, this site was closed, an alternative merger occurred with a slightly better arrangement at the newly built site.

My personal studies continued in addition with updating my knowledge on various aspects of midwifery and new nationally released guidelines from National Institute of Clinical Health and Excellence (NICE), Green top guidelines from the Royal College of Gynaecologist (RCOG). As far as I was concerned, I had to demonstrate excellence in the role and being conscious of my perfectionist approach to all things, I was determined to excel beyond my own expectation and ensure that my department was a shining example of a functional section within the maternity department.

This role has had its ups and downs and the downside being the insurmountable workload. The hours spent searching for health records to conclude tasks, starting work early with late finishing times became routine rather than exceptions. Administrative support was considered a viable option following a visit by an external body which materialised rather promptly. My role quickly encompassed a number of duties, encroaching into management. Before I knew it, my remit increased immensely.

So how was my family and social life progressing ? Had I forgotten myself in the name of sacrifice for the sake of the job? Was my focus one dimensional apart from pursuing the legal pathway? Work was enjoyable with opportunities to gain vast experience in a number of areas within this unique specialism.

I worked as an autonomous practitioner and commanded the respect of my colleagues.

Of course there were times of frustration especially when things became so routine that my dislike for futile traditionalism was beginning to show so clearly. Equally, I developed a good relationship with members of a significant network across the country and benefited from resources and shared information.

Being lead for the compliance with standards falling under the insurance scheme, was a huge challenge in itself and one which fell so heavily on my shoulders. Compliance with these set of standards came with significant financial gains and each year, the standards got much tougher. My first attempt at the assessment was successful and this gave me further confidence that I was on the right track and ready to face further challenges.

Well this success came with a price as simultaneously studying at law school, preparing for exams and working towards assignment targets landed me in hospital in March 2006. I was in agony from a left sided pain while finishing a law assignment on deadline day, in the library. I landed at Casualty in a City hospital with two young nurses attempting to administer a Morphine injection.

What I do recall is shouting at them to avoid giving me the second half of the syringe and loudly declared that I had not given consent for such an action. I cannot describe the feelings I experienced having the first half of the Morphine injection in my vein;–felt like I had lost my body instantly. A few days in hospital revealed nothing untoward and may have just been a matter of 'wind accumulation' as I had not eaten on time for a number of days.

Follow-up with a Gastroenterologist ended with a number of investigations–via the mouth and *derriere*–most unpleasant. I received a diagnosis of Irritable Bowel Syndrome (IBS) but not given any medication. Advice on diet was a standard template in my opinion and I was already aware of the foods which aggravated my body and those which made me feel real sick.

Certainly, I would not dare venture into the field of wheat for fear of going under the knife again to repair the damage that wheat had caused to my anal sphincter with recurring fissures. I hated chocolates, sweets, gateau and anything caramel or toffee. Bread and any wheat based products were a huge irritant for a number of years until this day.

Our boys were growing to be well behaved and respectful, bar the regular fights with each other in the house. I struggled to come to terms with their affinity for fighting each other in a hostile manner. We faced a few disappointments with schools and it goes without saying that I was well known for my no nonsense approach. Both boys were not allowed to sit on sexual education classes as we undertook these ourselves in the privacy of our homes.

We strongly believe that by teaching them ourselves, we would instil Christian values in the appropriate context. They were extremely keen on football and found themselves joggling both school and football activities. Thankfully, they were so compliant with the routine of attending church services and were certainly not streetwise. This was indeed a bonus as it was just one less stress.

Our sporadic extended holidays to Dominica were thoroughly enjoyed equally as the short breaks to Wales, Scotland, Devon and Bournemouth. We were certainly determined to strike a balance between work, school and recreation especially as our attempts at recreational activities such as badminton, Tae Kwon Do, Swimming and cycling were also sporadic.

As a private family, we tend to hold close to our hearts, a close group of people which we confided in as and when necessary and their support was incredible. Unfortunately a few non family members were certainly not displaying characteristics we felt were commensurate with our values and nature took its course.

Dynamics within my workplace were changing at a rapid rate while my husband's remained stable. In fact, he was promoted to a senior position which he felt was well overdue. I worked extremely hard in my role and brought about huge savings and changes, by creating and developing systems around safety and quality and earned the respect of my colleagues, the wider organisation and to some degree, our neighbouring

Organisations. I was not prepared to accept any destructive criticism and had always challenged any unwarranted attempts to erode or tarnish all my efforts in the name of safety for users of the service.

By this time, I was still undertaking the bulk of the administrative work in addition to wearing a number of hats under the one job description, which was not sustainable for very long. The turn-around did come and was happily welcomed, bringing much needed relief.

I surely did not recall signing up for secretarial duties which always brought back sour memories of my high school days. Imagine taking typing as a subject, battling to achieve a number of words per minute! YEK!!! A crazy idea indeed! This was akin to working like donkey for little pay. No sooner after the first review of the services and in response to the recommendations by the reviewers, I was assigned a secretary and would prefer not to give my opinion here.

Change came from the top in terms of directorship, an acrimonious relationship existed and we were singing from the same hymn sheet for some time. My sharpness and wit aided foresight to the extent that some proposals and changes came as no surprise.

I was confident that I was doing a great job and commended by reviewers for all my work. I sought counsel from one of the most senior male consultants who encouraged and persuaded me to apply for the higher post. It would be a travesty to allow a total stranger to lead my department; a department I had planted, fed and watered, only to be the same donkey for another number of years.

I will never forget the words of this Consultant; words to the effect–I can never see you working under someone new after you have put all these systems in place. This was the reality check. Although the consultation period gave me some reflection time, I had made my mind up from then on to apply for the Manager's post.

Ironically, my interview was scheduled for the day before we flew to Dominica for a four week break, to include Christmas. It was indeed a great time as I was comforted by the fact that I was successful at the interview and there were no competitors.

I can say I was pretty hacked off at having to prepare for such an interview for a job I was already doing, to be faced with a panel of five senior people; most of which were my colleagues. The interview came after sitting a half hour test which required me to state objectives and draw up an action plan. If only my heart could physically rip open to tell the full picture!

The holiday went well and during which time I received regular updates on the success and failures of interviews and the complete and utter discontent by those affected by the change. One thing I was assured of was the appropriateness of a good rest, at an appropriate time and in the best place. Maybe

I was saved from the flying rockets; considering the various outcomes.

My return in January 2008 was akin to a brand new start as some changes brought about by new ideas had begun to materialise. Was I to know that somehow, the turn of events would have magnified my strong desire to hasten the closure of this book? Time only could tell! Not even a strong and faithful Christian like me saw any of it coming. By this time, at the behest of the captain of the ship, changes were hitting me from every side. I was not in control of that ship as the helm had slipped and was transferred; depicting a further sign of things to come. Thankfully, insomnia which many complained of was truly unknown to me and night sleep was more than adequate to face another day, and another and another.

CHAPTER 5

CHAPTER 5

Moments of Pain

My husband and I were certain of no plans for further children but the maxim-'No pain, no gain' was lashing me from side to side in whichever context one wishes to apply it. As a mediocrity adverse person, striving for excellence in all my endeavours even within the workplace is second nature.

Achieving managerial position certainly came with its appendages. While I did not seek to be popular with any group or individuals, my contribution was to be of the highest standard, invaluable and of a certain class. I returned to face some demands and change to team dynamics. I was to face a huge challenge which took me rather by surprise. Thankfully, my characteristics are such that it is akin to taking no prisoners.

"Ethically speaking, I am not comfortable doing this"; was a vivid response which flowed so easily from my mouth.-"Why did you not do something about it?" Exercising equity is easy in my opinion but I am yet to come to grips with more than the naked eyes can penetrate or glance at so to speak. Why do I have to try and explain myself five years later, to members within the profession who feel hard done by due to the undesirable culture? Being in the minority and on a blatant continuum for several years, I certainly was not expecting royal treatment. Basically, I was in for a real bumpy ride but of course–no prediction on what ensued some years later.

Manager of two very distinct specialties was one COMBINATION. Wow! My passion for women and safety was top on my list, in addition to the well-being of ground floor staff. Believe it or not, this often felt like it clashed with other team members' priorities. I am a believer in leading by example and unless I am visible and supporting colleagues on the shop floor, I would deem myself as being hypocritical.

On–call shifts spanning over a twenty-four hour period were what we call in our colloquial speak–'nothing soft'. The impact of such a rota whether during the week or weekend was increasingly giving me a real headache for several reasons, but what was the alternative? Did I really have a choice?

My research and reading of several books, pieces of legislation, decided cases and guidance for health professionals further enlightened me to a level that only induced a degree of strength and courage. For example; I repeatedly asked myself–Is raising concerns a reality? If so, why as described by some, is there a feeling of endurance in a sort of lions' den?

Thankfully I had already been through law school and needed some other distraction in order that I did not flip so to speak, but also was capable of standing firm in the midst of adversity.

It was a mixed team in the true sense of the word, operating within two specialised fields. Some may well have by default landed in my team, others seeking for shelter of some sort while others genuinely had a passion for the specialism. Whatever the trigger or motive, I had my work cut out for me.

I thrived on being supportive, firm and fair, giving no one an excuse to judge me otherwise. Most importantly, the bedrock of my Christian faith was centred on equity and truth and I was determined that despite being in the minority, I would never compromise my Christian beliefs.

To a greater degree, I did not consider this new position a difficult challenge in terms of the nature of the job as by default, I was already undertaking the duties within this new role. As for strategic exposure, I certainly was under an illusion that there would be a sea change but undoubtedly this was a misplaced hope. The signs quickly became so painstakingly obvious that I had to apply a seat belt as it was going to be a bumpy ride.

I did not need to remind myself however of my ultimate goal which was not climbing the management ladder–certainly not! I had enough work to do under pockets of stressful situations. Undoubtedly, at annual appraisals, I would express my desire for experience to broaden my scope and gain a wider appreciation opinion but I am yet to come to grips with more than the naked eyes can penetrate or glance at so to speak. Why do I have to try and explain myself five years later, to members within the profession who feel hard done by due to the undesirable culture? Being in the minority and on a blatant continuum for several years, I certainly was not expecting royal treatment. Basically, I was in for a real bumpy ride but of course–no prediction on what ensued some years later.

Manager of two very distinct specialties was one COMBINATION. Wow! My passion for women and safety was top on my list, in addition to the well-being of ground floor staff. Believe it or not, this often felt like it clashed with other team members' priorities. I am a believer in leading by example and unless I am visible and supporting colleagues on the shop floor, I would deem myself as being hypocritical.

On–call shifts spanning over a twenty-four hour period were what we call in our colloquial speak–'nothing soft'. The impact of such a rota whether during the week or weekend was increasingly giving me a real headache for several reasons, but what was the alternative? Did I really have a choice?

My research and reading of several books, pieces of legislation, decided cases and guidance for health professionals further enlightened me to a level that only induced a degree of strength and courage. For example; I repeatedly asked myself–Is raising concerns a reality? If so, why as described by some, is there a feeling of endurance in a sort of lions' den?

Thankfully I had already been through law school and needed some other distraction in order that I did not flip so to speak, but also was capable of standing firm in the midst of adversity.

It was a mixed team in the true sense of the word, operating within two specialised fields. Some may well have by default landed in my team, others seeking for shelter of some sort while others genuinely had a passion for the specialism. Whatever the trigger or motive, I had my work cut out for me.

I thrived on being supportive, firm and fair, giving no one an excuse to judge me otherwise. Most importantly, the bedrock of my Christian faith was centred on equity and truth and I was determined that despite being in the minority, I would never compromise my Christian beliefs.

To a greater degree, I did not consider this new position a difficult challenge in terms of the nature of the job as by default, I was already undertaking the duties within this new role. As for strategic exposure, I certainly was under an illusion that there would be a sea change but undoubtedly this was a misplaced hope. The signs quickly became so painstakingly obvious that I had to apply a seat belt as it was going to be a bumpy ride.

I did not need to remind myself however of my ultimate goal which was not climbing the management ladder–certainly not! I had enough work to do under pockets of stressful situations. Undoubtedly, at annual appraisals, I would express my desire for experience to broaden my scope and gain a wider appreciation of operational matters. This all seemed like a paper exercise and purely repetitive as I was going nowhere fast.

Demands were increasing at a phenomenal speed for several reasons as when working in such a unique field; one eyeballs the distasteful and the few compliments almost on a daily basis. In many ways, I grew to develop a 'strong back' and was forced to adopt a soldier attitude at several forums, being particularly equipped with sound knowledge on a variety of topics and to some extent, using a defensive approach to drive home some crucial points or key messages. Ironically, thrived on seriousness and view laughing and joking as a weakness.

It was no laughing matter when on some occasions I was the 'odd one out' on points of discussion or decision making. As deflated as I may have felt in some of those cases, I never once felt like giving up but in fact (one may not wish to believe), this motivated me to wake up in the mornings to face the expected. In fact, I did not look forward to being on holiday as wanted to champion my own department giving support to the champion, support, advise, outshine and exercise uniqueness. Basically, I was not going to sit by and let anyone destructively criticise a highly functional and reputable section which I managed quite well.

My family life continued to do well and being involved in Christian activities was so inspiring. Regular gym attendances and swimming sessions were of great significance in maintaining my sanity and fitness.

My parents visited for brief holidays and certainly these times together were nothing but times of elation, laughter and enjoying each other's companionship. The boys continued to pursue football and were integrating well with school friends. My husband faced some uncertainty with regards to stability in his job of over twenty years but thankfully, he escaped all the chopping exercises almost on an annual basis.

Both boys in Bournemouth on a family holiday in 2010.
(Caleb (14)-left, Micah (16)-right

My desire for involvement in outdoor activities continued and I successfully completed the Street Pastors' training in the South of London over several months; giving up my precious Saturday each week. As a Street Pastor, I patrol one of the Town Centre in East London, while on night duty, at least once a month with a team of people from various churches in the borough. We reach out to those who are drunk, homeless and those of different needs and in so doing; we use the opportunities to spread the good news of Jesus Christ.

I was nominated as Chair of the Landlord Forum in my borough and of course that meant I am required to dedicate some spare time twice monthly; one to meet to discuss the agenda for the next Forum which I would chair with ease. This I fully enjoy as I found it a beneficial platform for expanding knowledge and experience in the field of property management, especially as my husband and I have developed such an interest for our personal benefit. There was a stilly determination to let nothing and no one keep us down.

My husband and I (2010)

Developing and co-ordinating a youth group (YOUNG AND SENSIBLE-YAS) was a challenge in itself but working with young people and facilitating them to be inspired to behave sensibly in such a precarious society was and still is rewarding. Gun and knife crime within the last five years was the talk of the town so to speak as the number of young people were falling victims to its fatal blow.

Ironically, I never wanted to work with young people as found them most boisterous and difficult to control. My sudden motivation was prompted during my Street Pastor's training in 2009 when I was convicted of my need to exercise some of my skills to help young people and having taken that step, I have no regrets.

Would a midwifery manager be so daring to get involved in community activities which would further pile on the pressure and could one cope with these extra challenges? The insurmountable pressure compounded by whatever else was part of the undercurrent meant I had to be super conscious and alert to cultivate the right balance; otherwise I would surely crack.

It was not for lack of trying to enhance my experience and exposure at strategic levels, but why did I keep trying? Interestingly enough, I was repeatedly being reminded that strategies for my protection were being applied by those who supposedly had the rule over me, as there were several demands for my skills and expertise at various levels; especially in areas which lacked a robust structure in my field of expertise. I felt this was an oxymoron in itself. In my opinion, such exposure would only serve to enhance rather than destroy.

Moments of pain arose in various forms and forums. As some may know me quite well, while I do not like to repeat the phrase - 'I take no prisoners', in many ways, this phrase describes me very well. On many occasions, my responses to what I considered extremely unsavoury required a number of drafts and sometimes a ritual of reading them aloud or passing them by a colleague I trusted and respected for their neutrality and impartiality.

Only a proportionate and a justifiable response would generate a more than reciprocal reaction–well deserved too! On no occasion was I rude or used profane language but maintain firmness, fairness and proportionality. I am a great believer of earning respect by giving respect and stopping inappropriate behaviour at the earliest stage.

As a citizen of the State with equal rights like any other within society and one who had earned a managerial position, was I not to be treated equally by colleagues irrespective of personality, faith and society? I was caught in a thicket. Was I honestly enjoying the protection afforded to me by the state?; exercising my own personality, faith and freedoms? In relation to patient care, health and safety, I was not prepared to compromise for the sake of gaining popularity with my peers. It is worth emphasising here again that I was coming from extremely lowly beginnings; but not prepared to be trampled over. Was I to exhibit jungle behaviour, bowing to all the whims and shouts of others who were of the belief that I should remain quiet even when things were wrong, unjust and unjustifiable.

Was it in my nature to allow the lowering of standards? I am well known for calling a spade—a spade and would argue relentlessly until I turn purple, in order to get my point across, irrespective of the setting; work, home, church, supermarket, bank or otherwise.

Imagine being refused experience in another area (even in my own time), as punishment for being efficient and following due process! This is Great Britain, flooded with all sorts of legislation, covering almost every aspect of life. Like the legal requirement to undertake an Equality Impact Assessment (EIA) on all hospital policies to provide assurance that no patient is being discriminated against, there are laws to protect employees and employers. I can only describe anything contrary as a *Malady like a raging cancer affecting neighbouring cells in its way!*

As manager, certain tasks and duties were unavoidable and of course, I was always willing to undertake these in the name of improving services for the benefit of all. However, mixed with that was the angst and sometimes animosity which ensued as I was seen as being different in my approach to undertaking those tasks. What was different you may ask? I was totally committed and determined, no matter what came my way.

Well, my passion for safety for patients, concern for shop floor staff, combined with a high degree of integrity, being extremely conscientious and having a compulsion to exercise my Christian characteristics meant I was in the eyes of many—eccentric; although this description was never openly directed at me.

It was virtually unacceptable to raise an eyebrow at apathy, incompetence and inappropriate behaviour.

My constant contact with staff and assisting them on extremely busy days were often frowned upon, as was deemed to fall under the umbrella of disempowerment. Only if this truly were the case, I would have reverted to my office within a second of greeting the staff and would certainly silence the mobile phone on those crucial nights and weekends.

My role was such that one was bombarded with reports of when things go wrong and when they did go wrong, they really did! I worked and tried so hard; maybe just too hard—I convinced myself. How wrong was I to think I was setting a good example for all to follow? I was so WRONG!

It was about 2009 at the peak of my career that the pressure increased further, to the extent that some were using my absence as a shield and buckler; a precious moment which could not have come quicker. It reminded me of my childhood days when I longed for Christmas which took ages to come each year.

Facing a catalogue of allegations in one case and not backed by evidence went to the substance of the entire discourse. Thankfully, I was (and still am) well known for excellence at my role and to a larger degree, an expert in my field and of extremely good character. I was well supported by the senior and junior medical staff of all disciplines and this was crucial to my work and central to my credibility.

I would be failing miserably if I do not take this opportunity to mention here that I had overwhelming support from the shop floor staff, with a constant flow of books, visits, telephone calls and other gestures (also from other members of staff outside my department). There surely were competing pressures and I was determined to persevere despite the many attempts to bring me to a low ebb. I knew that my promotion did not come from the east nor from the west, but from the Lord.

In the midst of it all, I never felt like quitting my job. Seeing Mum cry was practically unheard of where my boys were concerned and I held this position well until 2011 when one evening, I literally froze in my car from an episode of delayed reaction and what ensued was beyond my own comprehension. Was it time for another extended holiday?

A brief period of time off work gave me the platform to reflect on my future career and of course during that three week period, the degree of stress just heightened the adverse effects of a serious car accident I was involved in, in 2010. The car was a 'write off' following the acts of a reckless driver who followed me for some time after work. I remember the day very clearly when all others had left for their homes, and I stayed behind to assist the staff as they were facing staff shortages.

At the sacrifice of my own family, my priority was placed on the service needs. I could have disappeared at the usual time (although usual time meant a 9-10 hour day). My conscience would not allow it, but also knowing that central to my role was the issue of prevention and being proactive rather than fire fighting, being reactive and seeking for a cure after the fact. This accident left me with a left displaced rib, constant chest muscle and shoulder pains, difficulty lifting moderate to heavy loads and doing certain exercises, not to mention the regular cost for Chiropractic treatment which is still on-going.

My return to the working environment saw tears become a reality in the most unusual of places. Could I control those trickling streams whether in public or private? Questions pervaded my thoughts and for some time I sought refuge from key senior colleagues who gave their support as required but most importantly, I hid my problems from shop floor staff. Rightly so too, as one was duty bound to maintain integrity and professional boundaries. How long could one continue along this man-made destructive path?

Celebrating 25 years of happy marriage in 2010 was one huge achievement and one could not celebrate this milestone more sentimentally without the participation of my former Pastor who conducted the wedding 25 years ago, and my parents who were all flown from the Caribbean for this sole purpose. It was the worse day of snow I had witnessed in two decades.

Had someone prophesied that in the space of half an hour, Britain would be covered in deep snow, I would never have believed it could be possible. Although a few of our plans were thwarted and some guests were trapped in their homes, in the main, we had a brilliant time. We are thankful to friends and family who assisted and supported especially as my husband had to fly to Dominica just a month before, to attend the funeral of a close family member.

25th Wedding Anniversary (December 2010)

My parents and I at our 25th Wedding Anniversary

CHAPTER 6

CHAPTER 6

Timely Escape

The year 2011 certainly came with a bag of surprises which I had not foreseen despite the previous and lingering difficulties. I can only describe it as pure naivety on my part, expecting that I would receive lots of hugs and kisses, metaphorically speaking though; as it was already well known that these gestures do not go down very well with me. On no account was the situation helped when a similar rejection was being experienced externally at what I deemed as a place of refuge and sadly, some of it were truly interrelated to some degree.

External pressures meant that strategies for survival were merely heightened to keep heads above water. In an attempt to achieve the ultimate goal, I was undoubtedly the unknown and insignificant piece of the puzzle. Partisan behaviour also became so blatant that I truly felt insignificant and like a pebble so to speak. I went in to work each day, did what I felt was part of my role but where was the end product deposited? Basically, somewhere in the ocean, buried among rubble;—was my best description.

I was going nowhere fast. 'Snails pace' is an understatement. Just thinking of the several episodes brings goose pimples all over my body. What was really going on? For those who have ever experienced bathing in rough seas, just imagine the scene for a moment. The waves are hitting you from side to side and what compounds it is; the entrance of a gigantic tourist boat in your zone, passing some distance away from you but causing such a disturbance. Imagine the turmoil!

Communication deteriorated but my brain remained the bottle bank of all time. I concealed my emotions quite well among shop floor staff and their support was overwhelming. Where was I in the equation? What was really happening? Attendance at work was purely academic and I maintained professionalism at all times.

The question–"Who are you?" had never been so hard hitting like on that day and at that moment. It was like a dagger being stuck right across my chest, in an open forum. I literally and instantly felt 2 feet tall and getting shorter. It was nothing more than a feeble ploy to destroy every confidence, credibility, good work, progress and legacy created almost single-handedly. I wasted no time but did what was natural to me; and this was not turning the other cheek. Where was the other cheek to originate from when both had already been in use?

One cannot help but attempt to put the jigsaw puzzle together when pieces of the entire puzzle extended to those who had no business interfering but felt they were protectors. I then had a better appreciation for the real definition of blockages/blockades as I was going nowhere fast. I was in the middle of a real STORM.

Having experienced storms, tropical depressions and hurricanes both in the Caribbean and United Kingdom, the happenings were of a similar nature. There was confusion, periods of eruptions, flying darts, periods of docking and diving and quiet scenes with sudden unexpected bursts.

Akin to fishing expeditions were approaches and strategies. Thankfully, I was on guard and foresaw them coming from a distance, like the force of a hurricane which was preceded by a gradual whistling; building up to execute its final blow.

While my primary goal at work was not to challenge every living creature, I was not prepared to allow all my hard work to dissipate into thin air. I had developed and maintained systems and led on the road to accreditation success and saved money. I had done extremely well and better than most who according to a favourite St.Lucian saying; Ministers without portfolio.

I challenged their strategies with every fight in me; as an intellectual, black career woman who had gone through enough struggles to recognise Trouble when it is surfacing, just like being able to see a shoulder dystocia diagnosis for miles.

I was not going to be fooled by anyone whatsoever. I was ready for what was to come as I prepared my files, although cross references took most of my time. I am thankful to one Medical colleague who throughout the last year in office so to speak, listened to my concerns almost on a daily basis and I admire her for her wisdom, intelligence and diplomacy.

As determined as those planning the fight were, the pressure increased and more layers added to the hierarchy to the extent that I really became 'nothing'. One freelancer once barged into my office and issued her demand. A feeling of shock engulfed me. "My goodness me", I whispered to myself. Indeed, I had become NOTHING.

N - Nobody
O - Old
T - Tired
H - Haggard
I - Insignificant
N - Nuisance
G - Goner

But praise be to God- I remained SOMETHING in the eyes of God!!

I quickly received this vivid and kind reminder: I was:

> S - SOMEBODY; *graced with intelligence*
> O - *An Overcomer*
> M - *A Motivator*
> E - *One who thrived on Excellence*
> B - *One who will always Bounce back*
> O - *An Officer of Peace*
> D - *Determined to win the fight*
> Y - *Yearning always to do the right*

All throughout, I was constantly concerned for users and staff as on close analysis; I could not understand how those in strategic positions were placing them first. I knew that sooner rather than later, my time was nearing the end in that capacity as this was completely unsustainable. As a woman of integrity and full of godly fear, I could not sit by and allow what seemed like a show, a drama so theatrical that it would never hit the books of reality; no, not in this lifetime or the next.

I had stepped up on paper, but in reality, I was the step hidden behind the ladder and loyalty toward me by certain few waned and boy—did that hurt knowing my sacrifice. Words just cannot describe the feelings of betrayal. I had extended a hand to those I knew cried out for help in their own little world and as generous as I was, I provided a sort of shelter in a tough place. My theory that people deserve a chance whether they are of the highest intelligence or otherwise was robustly being put to the test.

Mini competitions erupted in the strangest of places and most cunningly too. I was driven to change my style of management for fear of being accused, but to achieve peace in my own niche created by self-help means and single-handedly. I was determined not to allow the hands of destruction to place a stamp in my territory. The war was on and whatever the course, I was confident that victory would be mine. My quiet confidence was not because of pride or arrogance but confidence in that, I serve a living God; one who keeps his promises and never fails his children.

I certainly was not going to join the competition to buy supporters, with gestures of edibles and niceties for the sake of it. My theory of: 'being firm, fair, intelligent, knowledgeable, respectable, respectful, professional and all-rounded is what counts', was my weapon and of course; total reliance on God.

The time came when all my parents had taught me from a child and the principles ingrained in me about not answering back and being timid became a blur. Instantly, I had a vision of an empty piece of land. I had the choice of filling it with rubbish, converting it into a tip or grow fruits and vegetables, making it a luscious place.

Of course, there was little time to think—very little time. A snap decision had to be made in the little time I had before me. It was a case of 'whatever happens'. Que Sera- Sera! What a hard hitting moment. The road to emancipation was opened in a flash.

The time had come to realise that I was no longer appreciated and the entire dynamics meant that my skills and expertise no longer fitted neatly within an environment which seemed to have lost its way in the eyes of local and national frontiers.

Of course, the entire problem grew into something so delicate and stuck out like a sore thumb for the Organisation. I believe in Almighty God and that no unfairness should go unrewarded irrespective of colour, creed or class. I was determined not to be another statistic but to turn this on its head to teach midwives and nurses like myself that it is important to remain professional at all times but equally important is to stand up against injustice and what does not feel right. It is a lesson for ethnic minorities, not to accept any standard below excellence, always analyse and where possible, challenge decisions before accepting and endorsing them.

In the natural realm, I then became a prisoner in my own home, unable to go swimming, go to the shops or attend certain events during the day for fear of missing those important calls. One thing I was certain of was that I would be on the winning side. The few months which ensued were the hardest of all in my adult life and I am thankful to all the staff and family members who lent enormous support for my situation. Support came in the form of gifts, visits and invitations and I am so grateful.

During this time, I had the opportunity to enter gainful employment as having then released my Curriculum Vitae (CV) to a number of firms and agencies, I was being sought for job opportunities. Opportunities passed me by and in my state of helplessness in this respect; I had no choice but to wait patiently. This wait seems like several years and the pains of frustration felt like that of childbirth. *As labour advanced, the pains became more intense.* My greatest hope rested in the fact that I knew that labour pains always culminate in a birth, irrespective of the method or the outcome.

I am grateful to God for allowing me to attend law school and my application of the law was so relevant here which gave me further injection of confidence. As tough as that period of time was, I remained composed and in fact, facing such a challenge infused me with daily doses of motivation. I could have developed a mental illness to the extreme that I could not function but praise be to God for his mercy and favour.

The entire ordeal culminated in the plan God had for my life and it was a good plan. He never leaves his children nor does he forsake them. I did not suffer in vain; no never. The keys to my breakthrough were perseverance, faith, belief, strategy, focus, strength, steadfastness and consistency, while maintaining my high standards.

Having finally escaped for good from what I call Lodebar, things did not suddenly improve and I certainly was not climbing any corporate ladders. Signing–on every two weeks at the Job Centre was something of the highest embarrassment, to the degree that I used strategies to disguise myself along that journey. While I was not attending the job centre for the purpose of collecting money; (the miserly £67 a week), my attendance was compulsory in order that I successfully claimed under my income insurance policy.

I tied my head and face with a scarf, ensuring that no one could recognise me on the way, in the street or on the bus or even in the Job Centre itself. How low had I stooped? Me? How did I get to that state? Did I deserve this? In all my questioning, I never questioned God, nor did I reject my faith or neglect attending church services.

I made hundreds of job applications to law firms, hospitals, large organisations and agencies in all different forms and attended a number of interviews. At one point, I applied for all types of jobs and was willing to take up an apprenticeship in construction. Working for the minimum wage was also an option and therefore there were no boundaries for me in the job market.

Honestly, I do not wish to return to that point where I would sit on my bed and write out several applications a day, receive numerous telephone calls from employers, prepare for interviews including huge presentations, travel long distances with negative results.

I detested the comments like;–"we feel you would not cope in a less busy organisation", "you are a completer/finisher aren't you?" and "you were excellent at the interview and we loved your presentation, but it was a tough competition". This was the trigger for me to form my own company.

Writing these two chapters was extremely painful and it took some time to achieve some of what I had hoped; closure to the devastation faced in the last two years before completing this book. Shockingly, writing raised further issues into the reality of the extent and gravity of my ordeal in modern day Britain. We hear of Human Rights and everyone being entitled to these rights but unless one is of a strong fortitude with resilience, a degree of knowledge, not thriving on popularity and pleasing people, irrespective of qualifications and expertise in a field; such erosion can only culminate in disaster, especially if one has no faith in God.

It was **a timely escape**, not only because I suffered no health effects in spite of the serious hard times I faced, but that it was a platform to realise my potentials. I am a skilful and talented woman who can face challenges boldly and confidently and it was not until I moved out of the situation that I formed my own company, being my own boss and enjoying the flexibility this new challenge brings.

As a director of my own company, I have no one to answer to, nor receive demeaning and demanding correspondences from those who embraced a platform for scoring points. Flexibility is a bonus and the amount of work I receive goes through a sifting process as at present it is in abundance. My stress levels are at an all-time low and I am enjoying every aspect of a new found freedom. In addition, involvement in various other activities such as learning to play the piano and guitar, church, youth and other voluntary work have kept me focussed and distracted me from meditating on the wicked acts by many in my past.

My story would be incomplete, had I omitted to highlight the positive points in the midst of some desert experience.

I am not a prisoner in my own home. I have the full support of my immediate and extended family. I have not fallen victim to any form of mental illness and have never found myself in a mental institution receiving treatment for what could have become an adverse outcome.

I retain a good memory. My integrity remains intact. My reputation goes before me. Rejected by some but respected by the majority.

A cancer diagnosis was excluded on two occasions in the past two years. My marriage of over 25 years has remained intact. My children are of good and godly character. I have not taken to drinking, smoking, nor taking drugs. I feel secure. I have not lost my confidence. I am employable. I am not rich but content. I have not lost my sense of pride. I am a self-motivator. My self-esteem is at an all-time high. I seek no approval of self-worth by gaining popularity with the world. I am worthy.

My grey hairs may have increased but my hair has never fallen off. Always seeking to maintain a healthy weight but never bordering on anorexia. I have an increased appetite for learning. I am assertive and confident. I remain self- disciplined.

Regularly, I repeat these affirmations:-
I am first and not last
My confidence is in God
My hope is in Jesus Christ
My faith remains Strong and Steadfast
No weapon formed against me shall prosper!

I have so much to thank God for at this stage in my life; (both past and present) and it is my sincere desire to challenge everyone especially all women coming from humble beginnings to be yourself, be professional, face challenges with confidence, accept no illegitimate and unjustifiable attacks in the workplace, be alert and realise your dreams. My childhood days were tough but my home environment was full of laughter and joy. I often revert to reminiscing on the good old days which I believe is good medicine for the soul. Much has gone on since then and my journey thus far has been one of mixed encounters. I can only hope that I never face another desert place of such magnitude. Having said that, I am better equipped with strategies which previously just formed part of my knowledge base.

I have **escaped in time** but how many men and women are still travelling along this journey feeling vulnerable, powerless and helpless with no confidence to take a stand and walk away from what seems to be a recipe for mental anguish and despair?

Some have already fallen victims and my story is one of courage for all groups especially women, health professionals and ethnic groups. It is in your hands to take action before it is too late.

I escaped in time!
But how many are still left behind?